THE CONSCIENCE
OF THE RACE

SEX AND RELIGION
IN IRISH AND FRENCH NOVELS 1941-1973

BRIAN O'ROURKE

FOUR COURTS PRESS

TECHNICAL & LEGAL INFORMATION

This book was typeset in 11 on 13 pt
IBM Press Roman and printed and bound
in the Republic of Ireland for Four
Courts Press Limited, 3 Serpentine
Avenue, Dublin 4.

ISBN 0 906127 22 X

For my brother Caoimhín,
whose year it is

I go to encounter for the millionth time the reality of experience and to forge in the smithy of my soul the uncreated conscience of my race.

James Joyce, *A Portrait of the Artist as a Young Man*

CONTENTS

INTRODUCTION

'We facilely talk about "English Catholic" and "French Catholic" novelists. I have never heard anyone talk about an "Irish Catholic" novelist': thus the critic John Jordan, who was not the first to make such observations. The term 'Catholic novelist' is, of course, one which pleases very few, least of all those so labelled; French writers refusing the description, for example, include Mauriac, Bernanos, Julien Green, Gilbert Cesbron, Pierre-Henri Simon, Paul-André Lesort, Jacques de Bourbon Busset and Jean Sulivan. Graham Greene likewise rejects the title, and the Irish writer John Broderick has this pithy comment on the subject: 'Catholic novelist, a most misleading term. . . . No one has ever heard of a Protestant novelist.It is only Jews and Catholics who are, or were thus branded: an interesting comment on the attitudes of the times'.

Be that as it may, one can feel some sympathy for critics who use the term to classify certain writers in countries where world-views vary widely. And, in the Irish context, there is perhaps ground for surprise at the implications of Jordan's remark. After all, not every Irish author reared as a Catholic has repeated Joyce's *non serviam,* and one might expect this fact to be reflected in the novels. And of course it is; several Irish novels testify in one way or another to their authors' Catholicism. Is the avoidance of the 'Catholic' label, then, an index of the critics' discernment? Perhaps. I should like, however, to put forward another possible explanation; it is that such 'testimonies' are, in the main, peripheral and incidental, and that there is a fundamental respect in which Irish novelists who have remained Catholic scarcely differ from those who have not. It is with this question, rather than with definitions of the 'Catholic novel', that I intend to concern myself in these pages. My main contention is that despite an obvious division at the level of *belief,*—the 'gulf' John Broderick sees between himself and Brian Moore—, there exists, with regard to one of the major central themes of the modern Irish novel, no corresponding divide at the level of *imagination.* The theme I refer to—it is also arguably the one most favoured by the French 'Catholic novelist' —is the conflict between individual liberty (particularly in sexual matters) and religious authority. Where this subject is concerned, Irish novelists of Catholic background, whether their relationship with Catholicism be one of fidelity, hostility, or uneasy neutrality, display, almost without exception, what I would describe, borrowing a term from a critic of Henry James, as a 'negative imagination'. That is to say that they seem incapable of imagining a harmonious relationship between self-affirmation and acceptance of the Catholic faith, still less between faith and sexuality.

This uniformity of approach to a crucial problem on the part of Irish writers of varying attitudes to Catholicism has, I believe, evoked less comment than might have been expected—perhaps because it has left most readers unaware of alternative modes of treatment. What I should like to do is to detail this Irish uniformity, and to draw attention to an alternative approach which is to be found precisely in the works of many French 'Catholic novelists'.

In contrasting the two groups of authors, I shall not be concerned primarily with value-judgements—literary or other; my aim is neither to proscribe nor to prescribe, but merely to describe; I feel that a clearer understanding of what the Irish novel—or at least one of the main types of Irish novel—is, can be helped by a deeper appreciation of what it is not. (There may be, in outlining the Irish approach, a risk of labouring the obvious, but I suspect too that assumptions about the normality of the 'negative imagination' may partially blind one to its very prevalence.)

My method will be, confining myself to the period 1941-1973, and proceeding not chronologically but thematically, to outline the Irish writers' treatment of different categories of characters and situations illustrating the sex-faith/individual-authority conflict, and to show the contrasting approach of some of the French 'Catholic novelists' of the same period who take similar characters and situations as their starting-point.

CHILDREN IN CHAINS

The particular Irish embodiment of the conflict I should like to begin by sketching is one that remains, as it were, embryonic. The predicament is that of the immature Catholic who feels oppressed by authority and/or by the sexual morality of the Church, and who, unable to take sin lightly, lives in a state of continuing unhappiness. The presentation is inconclusive: no real resolution is reached; the misery is the message.

Gerald Hanley's portrayal of Una Brennan in *Without Love* (1957) can serve as an introductory example. Timid, scrupulous, mother-dominated, Una 'feared always that she was not being pure, demure. She lived not far from the confessional box always.' Yet she can be 'annoyed ... with her religion ... why had she not been born a pagan? She could have gone to bed long ago with a man and satisfied this gnawing, burning itch which filled her.' The novel takes her to the threshold of marriage—one hardly calculated to fulfil her dream of a life of prayer in the flesh—but not beyond; Hanley is interested in Una primarily as neurotic virgin: 'she could not hold on much longer, she thought at times. . . . She was demented by the fear of pride, yet she was weary of virginity. At twenty-eight, she smouldered, and prayed.'

Another mother-dominated character figures in Kate O'Brien's *The Last of Summer* (1943), a pessimistic account of a clash between authority and self-assertion through love. Tom Kernahan's plan to marry his French cousin is subverted by his mother; though he 'wish(es) to God there weren't so many bloody regulations in the world', and has harsh words for the Churchmen who, at her behest, delay the dispensation, he succumbs to the influence of his mother—the real religious authority to which he will remain pathetically subject.

Similarly incapable of self-assertion is Diarmuid Devine, 'hero' of Brian Moore's *A Moment of Love* (1958). Unable to achieve sexual intercourse with a young Protestant girl, Devine blames his failure on his Catholicism: 'If I had been a Protestant, this would never have happened, he thought. I would have had my fill of girls by now, I would never have had to worry about going to confession.' Having accepted an expiatory caning from the girl's uncle, a fellow-teacher, and undergone a humiliating interrogation by the school's clerical authorities, he faces a future of continued sexual frustration ('How can I try again with another girl . . . without. . . worrying that I will fail a second time?') in his role as rebel manqué: 'He had not even been allowed to disgrace himself, to run off to Australia or Canada or someplace, . . . a man who had ruined himself.' Moore likens him on the last page to a cart-horse, harnessed and blinkered.

The hero of Patrick Kavanagh's *Tarry Flynn* (1948) can reasonably be compared to Diarmuid Devine. True, Tarry manages what Devine does not—flight from a restrictive environment—and for a variety of reasons, but it is worth noting that the agents of Tarry's humiliation include a domineering clergy, and worth asking whether his flight is not as much an escape as an assertion of self.

Tarry's chief likeness to Devine is his total inability to come to terms with love or sex. Like Devine, he is, in his own imagination, potentially a great sinner, yet he repeatedly shrinks from tangible opportunities: 'Some men could take life easy. Some men could dabble in sin but it didn't fit into his life.' He is equally indecisive where his more idealistic feelings for the 'breaker of hearts', Mary Reilly, are concerned. Though his cowardice causes him 'the deepest distress', he makes no progress. It is possible that Tarry's condition has nothing to do with religion: it is more likely, though, that whatever his purely psychological deficiencies, he is also a victim of the sort of fervid preaching which characterizes the parish Mission. He is certainly a clear example of inability to integrate a balanced approach to sexuality into a calmly-held faith.

The heroine of Edna O'Brien's *A Pagan Place* (1970) is likewise a victim of the horror of the flesh and the insensitivity of authority. Having been flogged by her father on suspicion of yielding to the advances of a priest, the girl cultivates, simultaneously, the urge to self-denial and the desire for independence from her parents. Both impulses are given an outlet by a recruiting nun who capitalizes on the girl's fear of hell to entice her to the novitiate. I quote the novel's final sentence:

I will go now, was what you said, hoping that she
would emerge from the house and have done with you,
but since no such thing happened you went anyhow,
and the last thing you heard was a howl starting up,
more ravenous than a dog's, more piercing than a
person's, a howl that would go on for as long as her life
did, and his, and yours.

The tone suggests that the narrator is no nun. The volte-face that we assume has come between the living and the telling, Edna Brien leaves unrecorded, content to let that howl fix the mind on the horror of a mind's multilation.

John McGahern also ends *The Dark* (1965)—or almost—with a howl: 'It seemed as if the whole world must turn over in the night and howl in its boredom, for the father and for the son and for the whole shoot, but it did not.' Ostensibly occasioned by the father's platitudes, the howl, exorcising the ghost of the Trinity, perhaps posits on the son's part, a new, more robust approach to the religion that has had him on the rack. Again, though, as in *A Pagan Place*, any clear break is in the future; what *The Dark* emphasises is the pathos of an adolescence made miserable by the conflicting claims of the spirit and the flesh, and more specifically by an absurd—and unchristian—spirituality which identifies sex and sin, and sees marriage as a high road to hell.

A similar pattern of suffering and implied disillusionment occurs in Christy Brown's *Down All the Days* (1970). But though the young protagonist is punished, in a nightmare, for his sins of impurity and his doubts about God's existence, the suggestion of a causal link between the two phenomena is not elaborated. What is stressed, for as long as the theme remains prominent, is that the feelings of guilt and shame attending masturbation are more powerful than the pleasure. The familiar motifs of the horror of confession and the fear of hell compound the problem, which is shelved, not solved, in the second half of the book.

One of the French contrasts to the trend we have been looking at consists of an evolutionary treatment of the type of situation we have seen presented *statically* by certain Irish writers: what the latter describe for its own sake becomes the starting-point for a development towards a more balanced, more authentically Christian mentality. This tactic is employed, for example, by Paul-André Lesort in *Les Reins et les Coeurs* (1946), by Pierre-Henri Simon in *Le Somnambule* (1960) and by Luc Estang in *Le Bonheur et le Salut* (1961). The theme of each of these novels is the adultery of a Catholic and his eventual repentance. The protagonists thus sin more resolutely than those we have seen up to now, but what is of interest at the moment is the extent to which their initial situation and outlook resemble those we have been discussing.

'I was reared in the conviction that I was condemned . . . to work out my salvation at the expense of happiness,' declares Laurent Seudre, Simon's hero. The remark would also be as valid for Estang's or Lesort's characters—Octave Coltenceau and Michel Estienne—as for the Irish characters we have met. Estang in particular insists on the ravages of an education inculcating fear of the flesh, and both he and Lesort describe the traumatic effect of the first sexual shock and the consequent crippling sense of sin. All three authors show their heroes suffering as much in married as in single life: two are condemned to celibacy, for different reasons, after a period, the other nearly so. Each feels subject to his wife in his spiritual life, and all three describe their condition as sclerosis. Their self-pity equals anything felt by the Irish celibates we have seen suffering similarly from sexual frustration and servile submission. The major difference is that the aim of Lesort, Simon and Estang is not to extract the last ounce of pathos from a sorry situation, but to describe this state as the first stage—we will look at others later—of a growth towards a more genuine, willingly-chosen Christianity.

A further contrast to the Irish approach is the inclusion, in the psychological make-up of a problem-character, of a streak of toughness, an independence of mind that precludes the sense of defeat. Luc Estang's characterization of Octave Coltenceau's future wife, Alice Lénarmont, is a case in point. After her first sexual sin, at seventeen, Alice, out of shame, shuns confession, defies her parents by dropping all religious practice, and hopes for an encounter worthy of an even more deliberate sexual indulgence. A period of external conformity follows, affording the satisfaction of deceit, till a confession, intended partly as a further act of defiance, becomes a turning-point.

Another obstinate and resilient adolescent is Serge Minardi, central figure of Jean Sulivan's *Du Côté de l'Ombre* (1962). Fascinated rather than shocked by his first glimpse of sex, Serge displays a corresponding insouciance in his first fleshly sins: 'Before even committing them, you already saw yourself entering a confessional, formulating the accusation, the great happiness of being freed invading you already. Before even committing them.' Contemplating marriage at eighteen, he is prepared to forgo the ceremony rather than recant his unorthodox ideas about the sacrament. Not surprisingly, he soon gives up practising. Sulivan's theme, though, is not the carefree revolt of a superficial adolescent, but his eventual recognition of, and regret for, his subsequent mediocrity.

Some other French writers describe a more direct passage from conflict to resolution. Maxence Van der Meersch's *Masque de Chair* (1958) is the story of a Catholic homosexual who, seeing himself 'condemned to perpetual failure, to relapse into vice until death,' nonetheless accepts the need to struggle, and dares to intone a hymn to hope which is one of the more attractive features of this rather over-emotional novel. However abnormal he may be in other respects, Emmanuel Ghelens is in one sense, of all the characters we have met, the one who most nearly approaches the Christian norm, by his ceaseless repetition of the role of the Prodigal Son.

The eighteen-year-old hero of Michel de Saint Pierre's *Ce Monde Ancien!* (1948), Gilles de Lointrain, finds chastity an intolerable burden; he avoids fornication through pride, and pays for his continence, according to himself, with an inferiority complex. Yet by his ability to provoke and then withdraw from compromising situations, to prove to himself that his abstinence is freely chosen, he shows a rather uncommon strength of character. The author is ironic in his treatment of Gilles, and severely 'reprimands' him for his pride, through the advice of a spiritual director. Yet he is optimistic with regard to Gilles' future and sees his eventual decision to take a shipyard job, in order to think less about his own problems and share the lot of common people, as a chance to attain a new humility and maturity.

This tactic of 'modified' irony is used also by Julien Green in his treatment of Emmanuel Fruges, an episodic character in his fantasy-novel, *Si J'Etais Vous* (1947). Green is hard on 'this old young man, sad and black like a sick rat' who 'oscillates perpetually between a yearning for virtue and the desire of the sins he daren't commit.' Yet when Fruges, weary of struggle, bitterly asks God why he created him, then realizes that to exist means to be chosen by God, Green's direct comment is that this 'sudden optimistic impulse . . . made up, perhaps, for such mediocrity'—a slim enough concession perhaps, but an index nonetheless of Green's optimistic imagination.

Much more significant, though, is Green's treatment of another character in the same novel, Elise. Torn apart by her love for her brother-in-law, this young girl goes through a struggle as pathetic as any we have witnessed. And though she disappears from the story at a time when she is suffering greatly, there are two elements which raise her conflict to a level above the usual one of the battle between piety and passion. Firstly, Elise's notion of God is more profound than any we have met: the legalistic vengeful God is displaced by a personal, approachable, understanding Christ. Secondly, Green introduces a mystical dimension into his narrative, describing occasionally Elise's consciousness of a 'feeling of incomprehensible happiness . . . . It seemed to her that she found herself suddenly in a region where nothing could reach or hurt her, with a sense of security too deep to be described or explained.' Green's hints of special grace necessarily modify our conception of Elise's predicament.

Are the Irish characters we have looked at representative? Are there no Irish novels which, limiting themselves to the 'embryonic' situation we began with, are not entirely pessimistic? Perhaps, but there is none I can think of which holds out hope for an integration of the conflicting forces, in the way that several French novels do.

Patrick Kennelly's *Sausages for Tuesday* (1969), a rather clumsy incursion into McGahern territory, evokes less pathos than *The*

Dark, but there is little indication of an evolution towards a mature Christianity on the part of the protagonist, who wishes he were a pagan.

In *One Small Boy* (1957) Bill Naughton's account of Catholic childhood tensions is less harrowing than the usual. His young hero, conscious of 'temptation everywhere,' feels that his 'whole life is lived on the very verge of sin.' Yet at thirteen he forms an easy relationship with a non-Catholic girl, whom he kisses without embarrassment. Achieving a balance between elements other characters cannot reconcile, he instructs her in the Catholic religion, and, in a touching and amusing scene, baptizes her. The harmony, however, does not extend very far, as his ideas about the sexual act indicate:

> No, not even when I'm wed will I do it. Ours will be a *pure* marriage. I don't care what the Church says—it's bound to be a sin. How can it be anything else? I'll be satisfied just coming home to Ella, having a kiss, Knowles's fried sausage for tea, together with pineapple chunks.

The novel is aptly titled.

Kate O'Brien's *The Land of Spices* (1941) stresses the beneficial nature of the relationship between a struggling adolescent, Anna Murphy, and a figure of authority, a Reverend Mother. The latter is hopeful of Anna's growth: 'She had been taught to be good and to understand the law of God. Also, she had been set free to be herself . . . Prayer would follow her, prayer always could . . . ' But the novel is generally non-committal in this respect: Anna herself feels that 'childhood indeed was over, that infinite lifetime, and . . . she was going out from it with no lessons learnt and no preparations made.' Incidentally, there is no question of Anna's having achieved a healthy integration of sexuality and faith; the problem simply does not arise, the great trauma she has had to contend with being the drowning of a younger brother.

The Fire in the Dust (1951) by Francis MacManus also contains some untypical features. The central figure is Stevie Golden, an English youth (living in Ireland) who intends to be a priest, and whose approach to sexuality is unusually healthy. His insistence to his schoolmates that 'a bodily act could be holy', however, earns him expulsion. He is disheartened by the entire moral climate with its multiple insinuations that 'People were rotten, suppurating, evil, mortal in their corruption to one another by contagion.' Tormented by a local fanatic, Miss Dreelin, over his admiration for Botticelli's Venus, 'he said that if he listened to (her) for long, he'd almost hate God.' He reaches a state of depression because 'he was afraid the religion Miss Dreelin and other people like her showed him, was right. If it was right, it was hateful.' When MacManus has Stevie accidentally drowned—through the unwitting agency of Miss Dreelin—he is expressing symbolically the impossibility, for a sensitive nature with a healthy attitude to sex, of survival in an atmosphere infected by puritanism. The negative side of his imagination has triumphed; there is no suggestion, for example, that the death has a redemptive dimension, as there is in Mauriac's account of the drowning of the central character of *Le Sagouin* (1951). MacManus's pessimistic view of the effect of puritanism is all the more striking for being that of a writer more influenced by his faith than most of his compatriots who deal in similar material.

I doubt whether MacManus's other novel, *Flow On, Lovely River* (1941), can be invoked as an impressive example of the sort of 'positive imagination' displayed by some of the French 'Catholic novelists'. True, MacManus does show, on the part of the girl who decides to enter a convent, an appreciation of human love, and on the part of the man who loses her, an acceptance of God's will. But, wary of expansiveness, MacManus plays down this acceptance, giving it expression only indirectly, through John Lee's dependence for consolation on Dante's line: 'And in His will is our haven.' The effect of this, combined with Lee's generally dour approach and his grim evocation of a bleak and monotonous future, is to make his stance appear at least as stoic as it is Christian.

TO BELIEVE OR NOT TO BELIEVE . . . .

We have seen, in some of the Irish authors' portrayals of 'children in chains', intimations of a future break with the Church. Before examining cases of actual revolt, I should like to make some reference to characters who find themselves halfway between belief and unbelief.

In *The Country Girls* (1960), *Girl with Green Eyes* (1962), *Girls in their Married Bliss* (1964) and *August is a Wicked Month* (1965) Cait (Kate) Brady and Ellen Sage, two of Edna O'Brien's heroines, are such characters. Both are products of a religious upbringing dominated by fear and suspicion of sex. Both drift from religious practice on marrying non-Catholics in irregular circumstances, and are unable to say for sure whether or not they believe: 'Not that she believed or disbelieved, she simply did not know', is the description of Ellen's state, and Kate finds it impossible to tell whether an Act of Contrition would be her reaction to seconds' warning of sudden death. Yet both retain sufficient vestiges of the neglected faith—particularly in the form of guilt-feelings about irregular sexual behaviour—to find impossible the carefree enjoyment of any supposed 'liberation'. Thus in each case, the relationship between sex and faith proves doubly negative.

In *The Barracks* (1963) John McGahern suggests a link between Elizabeth Reegan's relationship with a nihilist doctor and the loss of her childhood certainty in the faith. But the chief conflict that he explores in the novel is that between full adherence to the faith and affirmation of self. At twenty, Elizabeth decides that

If she lived the life other people lived, looked on it the
way they looked, she'd have no life of her own. She did
not want an ensured imitation of other people's lives
any more, she wanted her own, and with the wild greed
of youth. Safe examples that had gone before were no
use—her mother and father . . . —she could break out of
the whole set-up.

This keen sense of self remains, in later life, if not the cause, at
least one of the main features of her inability to come to complete
acceptance of the Catholic faith. She maintains religious practice
almost uninterruptedly throughout her whole life, and never
decides that the Church's teaching is definitely false. Yet while her
search for answers to life's mystery is carried out within the sphere
of Catholic theology, she finds, at several critical junctures, an
incompatibility between complete integrity and total acceptance
or submission. Going to confession before an operation, for
example, she wonders: '. . . *how could something so much the
living state of herself be state of sin?* She seemed to have grown
into it rather than fallen from anything away, she could not be
sorry'(emphasis added). Suffering after the operation, 'She
couldn't pray. *I believe, O God. Help my unbelief*, rose to her lips
and sounded as dishonest as something intended to be overheard,
she'd never made it part of her life, *it was not in her own voice she
spoke'*(emphasis added). If she resists the influence of the authori-
tarian priest who anoints her on her death-bed, it is because

Her thoughts had been with her too long, they had
changed themselves too often for her to want to change
them now because of another's interpretation of a law
big enough to include every positive position of honesty; and if her own truth wasn't within herself she
didn't see how it could possibly concern her anyhow . . . The whole of her vital world was in herself,
. . . it had nothing to do with what someone else
thought or felt.

Though her reference to a flexibly applied law seems to indicate a belief that the Church's teaching is broad enough to include views such as hers, McGahern nonetheless insists throughout that there exists, in Elizabeth's case, an irreconcilable opposition between dedication to a certain concept of the self and total acceptance of the Church. This insistence, according to our terms, partakes also of the 'negative imagination'.

On the question of a precise French contrast to what we have just seen, suffice it to indicate briefly that some of the French authors describe, on the part of their protagonists, a phase of doubt, uncertainty or atrophying of the faith, linked with laxity in sexual behaviour and a critical approach to conventional Catholics; they follow this up, however, with an account of a return to full belief. Paul-André Lesort does this in *Les Reins et les Coeurs,* as do Jean Sulivan in *Du Côté de l'Ombre* and Pierre-Henri Simon in *Les Raisins Verts*(1950).

THE BREAK

But now to those characters who truly lose or reject their faith. This step, as described by Irish novelists, is rarely the result of intellectual reasoning, it is, rather, an emotional reaction.

Michael Farrell's account of his hero's arrival at unbelief, in *Thy Tears Might Cease*(1963), is a fairly typical case. Martin Reilly does have a genuine problem of faith in trying to accept unpleasant events as God's will, but the real catalyst of his rejection of the faith is the crudeness of some of his superiors' insistence on the virtue of purity. His attitudes to faith and purity are of a piece: in both areas, encouragement and trust elicit a positive response, excessive severity induces discouragement. The crunch comes when, on the very day he has resolved that 'he would shame his own body no more . . . and no more think of problems which only theologians had the grace and training to master,' he is subjected by three priests to a humiliating inquisition about his feelings for a male companion and a female cousin. Convicted of sin, he is publicly punished by being made 'to stand in the place of disgrace' and it is there that he decides that 'he would beat them . . . and think what thoughts he chose in the solitude of his own heart.' Shortly after, we see him planning to edit *The Atheist Torch*.

In the cases of loss or rejection of faith described by Brian Moore, sex and revolt against authority are also prominent. Gavin Burke, in *The Emperor of Ice-Cream* (1965), completes his initially uncertain rejection of Catholicism when a proof of his personal worth vindicates him from the charge of failure pronounced against him by his father; having discredited that personification of all authority, Gavin judges that 'his father's world was dead', and feels freed at last from the religion which that world included. But this rejection of religion involves more than a revolt against his father's authority; sex plays a major role in his attempt at emancipation. At a time when he still feels a failure, and has not yet shed all traces of belief, he admits that 'the real trouble . . . is that I have sex on the brain, that I think about it every waking minute, day and night.' He resolves at one stage to reform, on all fronts, with his girlfriend's help, and decides that 'theirs would be real love, nothing to do with the dirty sex thoughts which teemed in his mind,' but then reflects: 'And Miss Holy Catholic Virgin here, . . . won't she lead you back to Mass and the sacraments and all the rest of it? Some agnostic you've turned out to be.' The recognition of the link between sexual laxity and the elimination of belief could not be clearer.

Moore is not specific about the moment of his hero's break with the Church in *The Luck of Ginger Coffey* (1960), but it appears that the break expresses primarily a rejection of the ideas of a preacher who condemns individualism:

> There's always one boy—Father Cogley said . . . who doesn't want to settle down like the rest of us . . . . He wants to go out into the great wide world and find adventures . . . his talk of finding adventures is only wanting an excuse to get away and commit mortal sins— Father Cogley looked down: he looked into the eyes of Ginger Coffey who had been to confess to him only half an hour ago— . . . .

As one critic puts it: 'The boy is to be shamed into conformity—the most certain way of . . . creating a religious outsider'. Ginger's comment years later—'I never could abide a bully'—is relevant. Is there a sexual component in Ginger's refusal of religion? We are not told the nature of the sins he had confessed to Father Cogley, but it is in connection with a disagreement in later life over Church teaching on sex that we are told: 'if there was one thing Coffey could not stand, it was being threatened,' and one of the things he most resents in the clergy is their intervention in the sexual lives of the laity. All in all, it seems clear that his break with the Church is the result of his aversion to a threatening clergy obsessed with sexual sin.

The heroine of Moore's first novel, *The Lonely Passion of Miss Judith Hearne* (1955), loses her faith when her prayers(principally for a happy marriage) go unanswered, but her full realization of God's apparent indifference comes only when she is confronted with the lack of charity of her 'friends' and her confessor: 'All men turned from me. And You, Father? You too.' Her summary of her predicament, after her disillusionment, is: 'If you do not believe, you are alone. But I was of Ireland, among my people, a member of my faith. Now I have no faith—and if no faith, then no people.' With a little more lucidity she could say: 'If you are alone, you do not believe. . . . Now I have no people—and if no people, then no faith'. But Judith's loss of faith also has more than likely a sexual as well as a social dimension. The extent of her sexual frustration is indicated by the almost hallucinatory intensity of her erotic fantasies, and while these are precipitated by her first doubts of faith rather than vice versa, the doubts are due to an exasperation with God, caused partly by sexual frustration. The novel's title, in fact, tells it all: her faith falls victim to her 'lonely passion'.

Despite the 'gulf' that separates John Broderick from Brian Moore, Broderick's imagination is as negative as Moore's when dealing with the conflict between self-assertion, especially through sex, and conservation of faith. His presentation of three ex-Catholics in *The Fugitives* (1962) is proof of this.

Lily Fallon gives up her faith on emigrating to London.

She had already given up practising her religion before she met Tom (her lover). The rigid set of hieratic beliefs, *accepted without thinking, without any real conviction*, because they were the custom of the country, had *fallen apart* at the first blast of foreign wind. . . . When the religious *facade crumbled*, most of the old, worthy standards had *dissolved* with it (emphasis added).

The words I have emphasised give the impression of the inevitable collapse of a superficial faith. Other indications, however, suggest a more conscious and voluntary activity: having 'broken with the rhythm that had moulded her and her people' (emphasis added), Lily has escaped from the 'certainty, the nullity, the watchfulness, the serpentine relationships of people who knew one another too well: the ultimate choice between hypocrisy and complete acceptance of the written and unwritten code.' After her break, we are told, 'There had been some moments of excitement; the slow, secret, miraculous discovery of the world of the senses; the intoxication of freedom; *the ruthless stripping away* of an ancient faith, a still more ancient superstition' (emphasis added). 'The ruthless stripping away' suggests a process considerably more voluntary than the falling away, crumbling and dissolving mentioned earlier, and the particular *sequence* of these 'moments of excitement' is surely significant. The reference to 'supersition' seems to concern her 'half-hearted, childish attempts to atone, that *pagan impulse* always especially active in those who have cast off a strict set of beliefs' (emphasis added), and these attempts to atone come after 'Brief bouts of sensuality, followed by self-reproach and a sharp sense of guilt.' It seems clear, then, that the 'ruthless stripping away of an ancient faith' which follows on Lily's escape from a restrictive milieu, is occasioned by the 'discovery of the world of the senses'.

Kate Fallon, Lily's aunt, an anti-religious ex-nun, boasts of the voluntary nature of her break with Catholicism: 'it requires an extraordinary effort of will. I managed it. . . . ' There is no sexual dimension in her case: her unbelief is the result of her experience of convent life; it is the lack of love she finds there that provides the basis of the theory of universal aggression with which she replaces her faith.

Broderick portrays the rejection of faith by another character, Hugh Ward, as being, like his IRA membership, a revolt against authority: he cannot accept 'majority rule . . . without hypocrisy.' When he tells Lily Fallon's brother Paddy, to whom he makes homosexual advances, that 'love' is the antithesis of hypocrisy, one suspects that his sexual leanings have some connection with his general non-conformity. And when Lily asks him why he will not leave her brother alone, his answer indicates that intolerance of his homosexuality has indeed helped to provoke his revolt: 'Have people ever left me alone? . . . It's majority rule, isn't it? Conform or get out?' His case, like Lily's own, illustrates clearly the opposition Broderick imagines between self-assertion through sex, and acceptance of authority and faith.

James and Gerald Hanley are two other Irish novelists who describe rejection of faith as revolt against authority. Gerald, in
Drinkers of Darkness (1955), attributes the agnosticism of his one
Irish character, O'Riordan, to a reaction against his mother's desire
to make him a priest. And his older brother, James, makes it clear,
in *An End and a Beginning* (1957), that Desmond Fury's unbelief
is the result of his mother's efforts to make his younger brother a
priest; it is her faith he rejects: 'I am sick and tired of having God
Almighty pushed down my throat. . . ., I don't believe in what she
believes in.' The same words could have been spoken by Mike
Brennan, central character of Gerald Hanley's *Without Love*: one
of the things he does say, at seventeen, is: 'All mother wants . . . is
that we go to Mass. She doesn't care about anything but Mass,
Mass, Mass.' His sister Una, much more submissive, admits that
'Mother . . . loved her children too much, and stifled them with
religion. That was what had driven Mike away.' Fifteen years later,
Mike 'loved Mother, yes, but he hated something in her too, perhaps her power to influence her children. Mother was Ireland's
shadow, the starving beaten hag, ravished but yet alive, praying . . .';it is difficult to believe that his atheism is a purely intellectual attitude.

The same is true of—and admitted by—a character in Paul
Smith's *Stravaganza* (1963): when his mistress is about to be ex-
pelled from the parish by the priest, his comment is: 'And then
the bloody man wonders why I'm an unbeliever, and why I don't
share his passion . . . for the rules and observances of the Chapel.
How could I take his worships and rites and ceremonies serious?'
(sic).

A similar case of unbelief caused by visceral rejection of abusive
authority is described by Thomas Kilroy in *The Big Chapel*
(1971):railing against the Church, Nicholas Scully says:

    I've no faith at all. I don't believe in anything anymore!
    . . . . How can you . . .? How can . . .? Something so
    rotten, so . . . That makes such wrong and suffering in

the name of virtue! How? How can anyone believe
in a God who rules the world like a Roman province?

A variation on the theme occurs in Walter Macken's *Lord of the
Mountain* (1967): the protagonist, Donn Donnshleibhe, has apparently been convinced by his war experience of God's indifference
to human fate, but at one stage he blames his unbelief on the in-
competence of the priests—'your failure is my disbelief', he tells
one of them—and the mediocrity of the faithful among whom he
has grown up.

In summary then, Irish novelists of Catholic background often
show unbelief resulting from an emotional reaction to crude authority and from the difficulty of sexual morality. More intellectual
causes are hard to come by; and if John McGahern shows Reegan,
in *The Barracks*, reflecting, on the death of his second wife, that
'You just go out like a light in the end. And what you've done or
didn't do doesn't matter a curse then', or Eilis Dillon, in *Bold
John Henebry* (1965) refers to a woman who 'holds that God is an
idea of man's, instead of man being an idea of God's', neither elab-
orates. And where unbelief is unaccounted for—as in Brian
Moore's *I Am Mary Dunne* (1968) and *Fergus* (1971), or (with reference to Baba) in Edna O'Brien's *Girls in their Married Bliss*—,
there is little to suggest that these cases are any different from
those we have examined.

One of the chief contrasts to the Irish authors' approach to the
question of the loss of faith, which can be observed in the works
of recent French 'Catholic novelists', consists of the attribution of
unbelief to intellectual rather than emotional causes.

In *Le Bonheur et le Salut*, Luc Estang has Serge Demonin, (a
foil to his believing hero) tell the story of his loss of faith. Serge's
motives in ceasing to practice are 'the opposite to those of many
adolescents.' He 'cannot even complain of being stifled by too-
rigid principles.' What incites him to give up religious obser-
vance at seventeen is the observation, not of his parents' hypocrisy, but of their sincerity, because, ever since an existential ex-

perience four or five years earlier, he has imagined religious forms to be *merely* forms, universally accepted as such. The belief-destroying 'illumination' he describes as follows:

> if others are struck by Faith, I was struck by unbelief ... it was an altogether intuitive, almost physical re-velation.. . . The shock of evidence: I can find no better definition of the phenomenon. Scales fell from my eyes. . . . Nothing made sense . . . God the Father . . . was . . . the principal victim of this sort of atomic disintegration. . .

In *Les Reins et les Coeurs*, Paul-André Lesort contrasts with his hero, Michael Estienne, a character rather less intellectual than Serge Demonin. Fernand Drouet maintains that his family up-bringing 'is bent on destroying in people the dispositions towards what is best in life'—i.e. sexual desire—and 'only offers a choice be-tween obedience and hypocrisy, at least to those not yet in a posi-tion to abandon once and for all the stifling milieu and its con-straints.' His predicament in adolescence is thus very similar to that of many Irish characters we have encountered. The manner of his break with Catholicism, though, is quite different: he seems simply to reach the conclusion that he has no faith:

> One must not . . . pretend that faith is given to or pre-served for all those who loyally ask for it. For if there is one game that he, Fernand, has played loyally, it is in-deed the game of faith. But one had eventually to un-derstand that that loyal game had been no more than a game. And then, how easily one abandoned the char-acter that one had been fashioning for so long. . . .

Other references to loss of faith for reasons different from those advanced in Irish novels concern characters whose subsequent de-velopment is more 'positive' than that of the two we have just seen. Jacques de Bourbon Busset, for example, in *Les Aveux Infidèles* (1962), has his narrator deny any connection between unbelief and sexual desire: 'At sixteen, I had put God in brackets because his existence bothered me. I told myself: "I'll look into that later. More important tasks call me. If I want to study this question more deeply, all others will seen insignificant." I turned away from God in order to dedicate myself, without remorse or scruples, to what I called action.'

Béatrice Beck, in *Barny*(1948), also indicates an intellectual approach on the part of her heroine:

> I thought it absurd of Donique to attribute my lack of faith to pride. I aspired to a God of a mathematical evidence . . . . It seemed to me that by conducting my reasoning with impeccable rigour, I should manage to prove to myself the existence or non-existence of God. . . . I couldn't live without understanding the meaning of life, or with the supposition that it had none.

Ex-Catholics figure prominently in Pierre-Henri Simon's work; Elsa Mailleri, in *Les Hommes ne Veulent pas Mourir* (1953) is one example, Noël Dussert in *Histoire d'un Bonheur* (1965) another. Simon makes it clear that Elsa loses her faith against her wishes and for intellectual reasons, but Noël's case is less straightforward: 'Noël was soon persuaded that the path to happiness passed through the enjoyment of desire; and it was indeed this moral conviction, more than the questions of science and history posed by his rigorous intelligence, which had turned him away from religion at an early age.' His case thus resembles that of several Irish characters, and the contrast to these which it represents lies principally, as we shall see, in his subsequent development.

The same is true of the hero of Paul-André Lesort's *Vie de Guillaume Périer* (1966). Guillaume's adolescent rejection of religion is unquestionably a revolt, in the name of freedom, against his parents'—particularly his mother's—influence. However, in the account of Guillaume's early life, Lesort—like Simon, with his reference to Noël Dussert's questions of science and history—gives his hero credit for at least some element of intellectual approach: Guillaume is aided in his reasoning by considerations of comparative religion and of recent 'scientific study' of Christ's divinity. Such things in themselves already indicate an absence of that 'negative imagination' which accounts for unbelief exclusively in terms of sexual frustration and/or emancipation from authority.

THE OLD MYTHOLOGY

We have seen faith rejected for the sake of independence and fulfilment. The sequel to that rejection we can thus consider as a relationship between unbelief and fulfilment, and the study of its treatment by our two groups of authors forms a logical extension to what we have been doing up to now.

The Irish authors' imagination in this area remains as negative as ever. For a start, they often show their ex-Catholic characters devoted to a cause or a pursuit linked in most cases with a resentment of Catholicism or Catholics that already augurs badly for their happiness.

James Hanley's Desmond Fury, for example, sees hatred of priests and the Church as an integral part of his socialism: 'He had always hated the word('Father'), and the cloth more, as all good revolutionaries must'; 'I've said I hate the Church, and I hate it.'

'Roger hated the Church. He hated it for its hypocrisy . . .', says the hero of John Broderick's *The Waking of Willie Ryan*(1969) referring to a former lover. Willie himself hates the Church and turns the last months of his life into a campaign of revenge against those who committed him to an asylum on account of his homosexuality.

Hugh Ward, in *The Fugitives*, explains his active attack on Irish Catholic society by saying: 'When you can't love, there's nothing left but hate.' Paddy Fallon, in the same novel, considers religion a major obstacle to the liberation of Ireland, and, referring to the IRA's cause, says: 'You've got to hate everything, sisters and aunts and all, everything. Nothing matters except this thing we're doing. . . . Christ, God, nothing else. . . . ' His aunt Kate's cause is denunciation of religion: when she remembers her sad convent days, 'The old woman's eyes glinted with a hard, fanatical light.'

Across that 'gulf' again, to Brian Moore: Judith Hearne, having lost the faith, is without a cause and without hate, but does feel resentment as well as loneliness. Ginger Coffey is not very definite about the cause which replaces his faith; the aim of his life is, he supposes, 'to be his own master . . . . To make something of himself . . . ,' but in fact any serious effort he makes in this direction is bound up with his resentment of the Church. Brendan Tierney, novelist-hero of Moore's *An Answer from Limbo* (1962), writes in order 'to revenge (him)self on the past' and therefore on Catholicism, which he hates: when he discovers that his mother has baptised his children, 'In that moment I hated her. She was my past, with all its stubborn superstitions, its blind emotional faith.'

In *Drinkers of Darkness*, Gerald Hanley may mean O'Riordan's 'studies of the universe' in his library 'filled with the razor edges, the broken idols, the flashing brightness of a thousand intellects which put the mind at courageous ease' as a revenge on childhood censorship which left him 'Night after night in the attic, poring over *The Messenger*, all other books locked away by Mother.' And hatred would be an accurate description of his feelings for one aptly-named writer encountered in childhood: 'Father Furness, the spoiled writer with the mind of a demon,' who specialised in depictions of hell. The hatred is more explicit still in *Without Love:* Mike Brennan 'hated something in (his mother) . . . , perhaps her power to influence her children'; having dedicated himself to a variety of causes—communism, fascism, anarchy—, 'He wondered if he was condemned to wander from one hatred to another merely because he could not be a good Catholic.' Eventually he suspects that his life of violence may be explained by a hatred of God: 'You could be so full of God that in your fight against Him you . . . hated Him. . . . Perhaps he hated God because He was there.'

The two sections of *Thy Tears Might Cease* which follow the account of Martin Reilly's revolt, Michael Farrell entitles, respectively, 'Initiation in Love' and 'Initiation in Hate.' In his dedication to the cause of Irish freedom, Martin is motivated partly by a deepening anti-clericalism, and hopes to help rid his country of 'the vulgarity of a love of God commercially coarsened to a parody of what it pretends to be.' He sees human love and love of God as opposites; priests, he feels, 'hate life, . . . they hate love. They must in honesty hate and fear everything. . . . Their love of God must simply become hate to life . . .'; consequently, they are 'all that he most hated and despised.' And the ultimate target of his resentment—as of Mike Brennan's—is a supposedly non-existent God: 'O hateful God, I defy You.'

Edna O'Brien also associates the ideas of hate and a non-existent God in *Girls in their Married Bliss* when she has Baba, revolting against the feminine condition, exclaim: 'O God, who does not exist, you hate women, otherwise you'd have made them different. And Jesus, . . . You hate them more. . . . Abandoning women.'

And, to complete the catalogue, we may notice another variation, in Thomas Kilroy's presentation of Nicholas Scully. The ex-seminarist is asked, by the dissident priest whose cause he champions, to tell his story. 'So Nicholas did. . . . As he went on, dressing the story, he hated himself, he hated the priest for provoking him to it.'

The second negative feature of the sequel to revolt, as described by Irish writers, is the frustration encountered in the dedication to a cause. This is the case even with characters whose rejection of the faith is so final that they cease to feel its influence, but more often the frustration is due precisely to such influence.

This is true, for example, of Brian Moore's account of Ginger Coffey's crisis of confidence. Ginger's failure to make something of himself leads him to suspect that Father Cogley may have been right: 'maybe God had lain in wait for him all these years . . . until now he was stranded. . . ?' However, he later accepts the blame for his own failures, and, having tried to make up for them by a disinterested act, is rewarded not only by the fidelity of his wife but also by a 'mystical' experience which, teaching him 'the truth' and giving him a new confidence in life, apparently frees him finally from fear of Father Cogley's vengeful God. And yet there is a three-fold irony here: firstly, the selfless act which earns him emancipation is inspired by a desire to imitate Christ, and his trial re-enacts Christ's sufferings in several details; secondly, his 'mystical' experience displays many strictly evangelical features; and, thirdly, the attendant 'truth' which appears to set him free from his Catholic past brings him closer to agreement with Father Cogley than he appears to suspect: 'He had tried: he had not won. But oh! What did it matter? He would die in humble circs. . . : it did not matter. There would be no victory for Ginger Coffey, no victory big or little, for . . . he had learned the truth. Life was the victory, wasn't it? Going on was the victory. For better or for worse. . . . ' Is this not, after all, a heeding of the preacher's warning that 'that class of boy (who) is unable to accept his God-given limitations . . . (will) sink in this world. . . . '? Ginger's gain in realism—in renouncing his dreams and resigning himself to mediocrity —may be healthy, but his liberation from Father Cogley is largely illusory.

A similar paradox characterizes Moore's treatment of Brendan Tierney, in *An Answer from Limbo*. The publication of Brendan's first story is an important step in his liberation: 'I was freed. . . . I was baptized in a new communion. . . . I left my parents' world forever.' Yet, seven years later, he asks: 'have I really been freed? '; like Ginger Coffey, and Gavin Burke, he has to complete his emancipation by a proof of his personal worth; in his case, the proof will be the publication of his first novel. But though his writing is meant largely as an anti-religious act, he is incapable of thinking of it in any but religious terms: 'I've made writing my religion . . .'; 'My book for me . . . is the belief that replaces belief. . . .' In fact it seems that his book does not so much replace belief as obscurely express it; knowing he is writing for *someone* and being unable to identify that someone, he asks: 'Who then? Some old Dog-God Father who will look down and tell me he is well pleased?' Besides, seen as a revenge on his Catholic past, his effort backfires: his novel does indeed cause the death of his mother, who 'is' his past, but her death becomes for him the occasion of his most explicit suspicions that the faith he has rejected may be true, as well as of a radical questioning of the validity of his literary endeavours. In short, his hope of liberation from religion through literature is frustrated by an ineradicable religious sensibility and by ironical external events.

Back to Broderick again; his fugitives too flee in vain. Lily Fallon, in *The Fugitives*, rather than having a cause to replace her faith, 'was left with nothing but an empty day-to-day pragmatism and a vague sense of guilt'. Being 'impossibly romantic,' though, she seeks happiness through love, but her sense of guilt sharpens after her bouts of sensuality. That this guilt is no mere 'pagan impulse', but springs from a residue of a very specific religion, is proved by one crucial incident: after an impersonal sexual encounter, she has to pass under an image of the Blessed Virgin, and 'out of the past, conjured up by the shining figure, the words of the litany came terrifyingly back into her mind. Tower of Ivory, House of Gold, Ark of the Covenant. . . . The words haunted her like . . . an echo that would never fade from her mind.' Broderick's comment is: 'She had never discovered . . . that virtue is a great deal more ruthless than lust'; his meaning is, presumably, that her efforts at a 'ruthless stripping away of an ancient faith' are powerless to dislodge certain tenacious remnants. They are, as it happens, just those remnants most calculated to vitiate her quest for happiness through sexual love.

Broderick shows Lily's brother, Paddy, to be a victim of the sort of irony Brian Moore sees in Brendan Tierney's fate. The key idea that sustains Paddy in his effort to destroy the Irish social and religious set-up is that of suffering, and the author guarantees as accurate the analysis of Paddy's attitude supplied by his aunt Kate; displaying what Broderick calls 'shrewd . . . insight', she says:

> Paddy was brought up as a Catholic. From the time that he could speak it was drummed into him. It's not something that many people ever really escape from . . . I managed it; but Paddy hasn't . . . he really wants to sacrifice himself, to suffer. . . . It's all part of something that Paddy remembers, not so much with his mind as with his heart. The whole of Catholicism is based on the need to atone, to suffer, to sacrifice. . . . There are other things, of course, but that is the fundamental thing. And that is what he has remembered. He wants to destroy himself.

(He succeeds, in fact.) But Kate herself is not exempt from this irony. Broderick tells us, *à propos* of her comments on Paddy:

> It did not occur to Aunt Kate . . . that she was in fact speaking of herself. The old woman did not see in her bare room a reflection of the convent cell; in her black belted dress a faded copy of the habit she had discarded; in the proud ascetic life she led, the rule of the Order she had left.

The paradox does not involve externals only: when Hugh Ward tells her that Paddy blames her for his loss of faith, she is shattered, and the words of the De Profundis which she mutters between sobs testify to a remorse that is a direct contradiction of her principles—'I do not believe in belief'—and of her habitual conduct.

Michael Farrell, like Broderick, shows repudiation of the faith ending in self-division. Martin Reilly, seeing that the revolution he has dedicated himself to has left intact the religious system he wished to destroy, is forced to agree bitterly with AE that 'We become like what we hate.' More importantly, he fails to forge a new independent identity outside the Church: despite his vigorous rejection of 'The whole fantastic caboodle. . . . A fairy-tale to make one happy as a boy', the faith continues to be a 'bell note which even he could not entirely silence in his heart.' Eventually, oppressed by 'the eternal silence which had terrified so many before and since Pascal', he wishes to believe again, and rejects 'all explanations that explained nothing, . . . all the clever words with which reason had fortified the prior reasons of his heart.' But he finds that 'to disbelieve he would have to deny one-half of himself, and to believe deny the other half.' And Farrell shows no healing of the breach.

Of all Irish novelists, Gerald Hanley is perhaps the one whose description of the frustration of the will to disbelieve is the most uncompromising. In *Drinkers of Darkness*, he shows O'Riordan, 'the great agnostic, the fearless one', discover, with the approach of death, that 'his selfish agnostic courage . . . had never truly sustained him, . . . had never won over the childhood and the centuries of prayer.' His 'studies of the universe' have been in vain: 'I feel certain that there is a plan in this universe which defeats all my reading and thinking.' But more importantly, what his agnosticism succumbs to is his childhood fear of hell: 'Courage? . . . his mind . . . had never quite recovered from Father Furness's works. . . . ' If he confesses for the first time in thirty years, it is because 'his ancient religion . . . (had) overcome his lifelong scepticism . . . ';'mother had won, the mother of holy ruined Ireland. The family saying the rosary at night had triumphed.' Yet his confession brings no comfort, for he feels no faith: 'He lived

now in two worlds, of doubt and the will to believe, and now both
sought to give him relief and could not calm him.' He remains
divided, getting the worst of both worlds, feeling 'no relief, no
forgiveness, no sight of God, no faith, nothing,' yet suffering the
effects of his earlier belief just sufficiently to make him 'kneel
down by his bed, a child broken from a wondering man,' praying
for fear of hell, because 'Bigger than Bwana Freud was the animal
with no shape which waited to cry in terror, which made a savage
meal of reason when the keeper was losing the war with mystery.'

Defeat and division are also the lot of Mike Brennan in *Without
Love*. Brennan discovers the futility of his various causes: 'I hate
the world as it is . . . But no one will ever change it.' What troubles
him more, when he finds himself in danger of imminent death, is
the suspicion that his hate may be the hate of a really existing God,
for, after years of calm killing, his Catholic conscience accuses
him: 'his own heart was eating him alive, . . . his superstitions, and
the deep ferment of God put into him in his childhood, were
gnawing his spirit like pain.' Freud is as powerless in his case as in
O'Riordan's: 'Guilt-complex. Mother-fixation. Infantile paralysis
of the soul. He could call it anything out of the jargon-list, but
when the longing to kneel down came it was bigger than the
jargon-list could describe.' He attributes his desire to believe again,
at times to fear of death, at times to God's direct influence, and
while his assertion of belief can on occasion be extreme—'It's
because I believe, that I've come to a standstill. I don't want God
but I can't get rid of Him. He's here, eating me'—he also suspects
that 'What he thought was a hunger for God might be . . . a desire
to escape . . . ', to be free of a horrible past. He achieves no resolution in the interval before his sudden death. His tragedy—like
O'Riordan's, and even Martin Reilly's—is that he feels the effects
of his faith too much to remain carefree and too little to attain
peace.

For an entirely different account of the sequel to loss of faith,
we can look to the works of four French authors: Pierre-Henri

Simon, Béatrice Beck, Paul-André Lesort, and Jacques de Bourbon Busset.

Arthur Emery, hero of *La Sagesse du Soir* (1971), Elsa Mailleri, in *Les Hommes ne Veulent pas Mourir*, and Noël Dussert, in *Histoire d'un Bonheur* are three of Simon's ex-Catholic characters whose agnosticism does not exclude traces of Christian sensibility. In each case these are willingly accepted, being a source of encouragement rather than condemnation, since their moral lives are lived along lines that are partly Christian—both Elsa and Noël in particular, have devoted themselves to a humanistic service of others. Elsa's belief in the probability of God's existence sustains her in her efforts because she is aware of the limitations of material well-being and accepts that life is worthwhile only 'on condition that it opens out onto something worth more than itself, otherwise it is cruel and stupid.' Noël is quite trenchant in his refusal of Catholic dogma, but retains a certain sympathy with religion. He believes that his effort to build a more human world pleases a probably-existing God, and when the horror of war and deportation reveals to him 'the defeat of man', he receives what seems to be a consolation from Christianity: as he is dying, a vision of Calvary flashes across his mind. 'Love and suffering, mystery of the Cross!' is one of his subsequent reflections, and the last index of thought on his part is: 'he wished to say "My God!" ' The least one can say of his case is that the influence of his childhood faith is no hindrance to his conquest of balance and fulfilment outside the Church, and provides a useful consolation in his dying moments. It is also possible that Simon is suggesting that he dies once more a believer.

Béatrice Beck's character, Barny, dedicates herself to Communism for a period after losing her faith, but for some time at least her agnosticism accommodates love for the person of Christ. In a later novel, *Léon Morin, Prêtre* (1952), she is again assailed by the metaphysical questions which had occupied her in adolescence, and, through the influence of the priest who gives the novel its title, is converted back to Catholicism.

The hero of Paul-André Lesort's *Vie de Guillaume Périer* resembles, for a period, many Irish characters we have met, in having a 'cause' which is linked with hostility to the rejected religion: Guillaume wants his love for his ex-Lutheran mistress to be an existential refutation of Christianity. Paradoxically though, their love becomes 'a kind of religion of which we ourselves were the legislators.' His later meeting with the woman he eventually marries marks however an entirely new departure: her free commitment to him corrects the false notion of freedom in the name of which he has maintained his revolt against the religion of his parents. It is this repudiation of his earlier reasoning, together with the realisation that his wife's gift of herself is ultimately God's gift to him, which leads him back to full acceptance of Catholicism. Lesort's account of Guillaume's transformation is thus the most striking contrast we have so far encountered to the Irish authors' insistence on the incompatibility of human love and love of God.

Jacques de Bourbon Busset's description, in *Les Aveux Infidèles,* of the turning-point in his narrator's life, is remarkably similar to what we have just seen. Having begun to suspect the possibility of God's existence, the narrator is affected by the attitude of his wife, who has 'entered into passion as into religion,' and who claims that her love for him forces her to believe in immortality: 'At first, I was convinced that your roles excluded each other, that one had to choose between what the books call divine love and human love. As it turned out, every point you scored helped the Suspect, and vice versa.' Eventually he has the impression 'not merely that you had entrusted yourself, but that you had been entrusted to me. Once and for all, by someone other than you. . . . ' That 'someone' he concludes to be Christ, because his wife's love has made the Gospels come alive for him. Having grappled with some philosophical problems, he comes to full acceptance of Church teaching. In fact his position represents a

double contrast to that of many Irish characters: not only does
human love direct him towards—rather than away from—God, but
also the human side of the Church, often a scandal, is for him an
encouragement:

> I was no longer so presumptuous as to recoil before the
> sometimes too human face of the Church. On the con-
> trary. . . . The Church implants the true in the real. A
> truth rooted in life was what I had always been seeking.
> And so, what was previously an obstacle became now a
> reason to believe. I verified the mysterious law of the
> roundabouts which are short-cuts, of the paradox which
> is truth, of the rule which is freedom.

A final word before leaving this topic: is there nothing in the
works of Irish writers less negative than the accounts of unbelief
embittered by hate or troubled by the resilience of 'the old myth-
ology'? Very little. Eilis Dillon, in *Bold John Henebry*, describes
the passage of Elizabeth Henebry from a life of unbelief to one of
genuine religiousness, but she makes it clear that the change is
caused by the lack of happiness experienced in marriage: the re-
lations between love and religion thus remain negative. In Walter
Macken's *Lord of the Mountain*, Donn Donnshleibhe says he
might be converted if he saw one person practising what he is
supposed to believe. When the rape of his daughter dashes his
hopes of constructing an earthly paradise, his neighbours' concern
for him restores his faith in people, and the novel's final sentence
shows him looking forward eagerly to the christening of his second
child. Macken may or may not be hinting at a possible return to
belief, but in itself the suggestion of a believing community's
positive influence on an ex-Catholic is somewhat of an exception
in the Irish context.

THE TWO LOVES

In our consideration of the Irish novelists' treatment of the sex-faith/individual-authority conflict in its 'embryonic' state, we saw the suggestion of either continued frustration or future revolt. Having since studied works in which the possibility of revolt becomes a reality, we can now turn, in the absence of more optimistic material, to novels in which the theme of frustration is developed further. For if growth towards a healthy integration of sexuality and Catholic morality is foreign to the Irish novel, the negative imagination is at home in evoking the aberration of puritanism.

Kate O'Brien, in *Music and Splendour* (1958), tells how Marie Brunel, a Parisian singer, is happy to live in breach of her Catholicism with her lover until she learns he is an ex-priest. With the discovery comes what he calls 'The change of beauty and love into some kind of medieval, witch-driven fury . . . , ' and she enters a convent where she becomes 'ascetic even to exaggeration,' but fails to achieve happiness or peace; years later, the use of a Spanish phrase picked up from her lover, can bring out 'some desolate quality in (her) voice.'

In Benedict Kiely's *Call for a Miracle* (1950) the beautiful Christine is happy with having a lover till the comments of a priest remind her of her childhood faith. Then, telling her lover, by letter, 'When I'm put to the test I'm just a pious woman as my mother was before me. I'm prepared to believe what the priest tells me and I'm afraid of hell when I die,' she flees to her home town, where she foresees herself 'becoming its most respectable old maid. . . . In some ways it's a worse death than entering the convent because in a convent the nuns have some sort of common purpose. Old maids in a small town have only their bitter tongues and their rosary beads in common.' No more optimistic prospect seems to occur to her or to the author, who sees her destined to harden in her view of others as well as of herself; as the lover—for all practical purposes, Kiely's spokesman—puts it: 'Christine saying her prayers in a quiet town will deliberately forget Dublin and the people who pass through Dublin on the way to hell.'

James Hanley portrays, in one of the secondary characters of *An End and a Beginning*, the sort of woman Christine might become. Winifred Fetch, after bouts of sensuality with her employer—'I've seen my tiger leap in a man's room, and I was all blindness and fire, and my common sense tossed into the very air about me'—feels remorse on account of the latter's crippled wife: 'And I learned to curse my flesh; I tied my tiger down.'

Like Christine, she fears 'The places my tiger would have led me,' and, never thinking of any possible *moral* use of sex, settles for an austere spinsterhood. There is a certain quasi-comic, as well as pathetic, note in the intensity of Hanley's descriptions of her subsequent lifestyle—her room, dress, spiritual reading, pious activity and prayer. Examples of the last-mentioned will illustrate:

> Day in and day out, through week and month and year, Miss Fetch sat and read, made vows and resolutions, worked for the Church, for the heart of it, and for the extreme fringes of it, in the heathen country, the hot desert, the pestilential places, the jungles, the Arctic wastes . . . . by the iron law of her own making, . . . she . . . said her prayer for the damned and cursed of Ireland, and the army of the ignorant that chattered to strange gods in the jungles of Africa . . . she . . . put on the cold nightdress that carried with it the chill and the penance of leather. . . . She . . . (lay) on her back in the iron bed, and . . . composed her body for the sheet, and her soul for the journey of the night. The beads . . . clung to the bone, entwined and held fast the hands, the lips . . . closed on always remembered words, the eyes upon the dying day.

The tiger has been tamed, but the keeper is a corpse.

Death stalks through Francis MacManus's *The Fire in the Dust* too, in the person of Miss Dreelin, whose fanatical puritanism symbolically kills the sole representative of a healthy attitude to sex. 'Tall and black and erect as a Requiem candlestick,' she presides over a tomb-like shop of religious objects, and makes forays into the world to condemn and convert. MacManus attributes her puritanism to an education that made her 'suspicious of passion, horrified by it, and contemptuous of the body', rather than to a reaction to any specific sexual incident. With questionable psychology, he shows her becoming infatuated with the widowed father of her eventual victim; significantly though, even this new acquaintance with the feelings is powerless to modify her hysterical approach to sex.

A variation on the Puritan theme is provided by Brian Moore in *An Answer from Limbo*, in his presentation of the hero's mother. Mrs Tierney feels responsible for the loss of a seminarian's vocation, and remains haunted for thirty years by the guilt of the sexual incident involved. She sees the various sufferings of her life as direct punishments for her fault, meted out by an unforgiving, vengeful God: 'He paid me back . . . all that's happened since . . . all that is paying me back. . . . The priests are wrong: You are not all-forgiving. You never forgive.'

A further variation is to be found in Richard Power's *The Land of Youth* (1966), which also describes the negative consequences of a seminarian's yielding to the attraction of a woman. When Barbara refuses to marry Padraig, who has left the seminary on her account, their relationship degenerates into a life-long battle, with disastrous consequences for both. Though Barbara's eventual vision of the land of youth—omen of a happy death—somewhat palliates the harshness, the overpowering impression is one of two ruined lives and of a wedge driven deep between human love and religious faith.

In the works of some of the French 'Catholic novelists', we find a number of manifestations of a positive imagination with regard to the Puritan theme. One of these consists in a description of the 'humanisation' of a Puritan.

Mauriac's account of Brigitte Pian's transformation, in *La Pharisienne* (1941), is a case in point. Afflicted by a remarkable horror of the flesh, Brigitte is eventually led towards humility by scruples and repentance. A period of indulgent interest in human passion ensues, causing laxity in her spiritual life; this, however, is paradoxically remedied by her falling in love with her doctor, with a passion which is 'fierce, exclusive, and . . . happy, fulfilled.'

Luc Estang describes a similar process in *Que Ces Mots Répondent*. Alice Coltenceau(née Lénarmont), after an adolescent lapse, pursues a path of hardened 'virtue', accepts marriage as a sacrifice and soon imposes a régime of celibacy on her husband, remaining for him an 'unknown woman, . . . cold beauty . . . untouchable spouse.' When he flees with a mistress, she is brought to recognise her inadequacy; when he returns, she welcomes him, and after their first night together, finding herself freed from the shame of the body, she formulates the equation: 'After all, to love is to pray.'

In *Le Somnambule* and *Les Reins et les Coeurs*, Pierre-Henri Simon and Paul-André Lesort, respectively, portray characters whose role corresponds to that of Alice Coltenceau, in so far as their unsatisfactory performance as wives drives their husbands to adultery. The approach of these authors also is considerably more nuanced than that of most Irish writers. Simon, for example, is at pains to have his hero reiterate the undeniable qualities, and recognize the genuine love of the wife he has deserted in search of a more exalted happiness. And though Lesort's hero resents the apparent ease with which his wife has accepted the continence imposed by the danger of a further pregnancy, and accuses her of being deficient in desire, both he and the author later correct this impression. Besides, when Michel returns after his adulterous escapade, it is Andrée who provokes a renewal of physical intimacy, desiring to 'set Michel free, or die,' and knowing that, because of the danger to her life, she may have 'to die, perhaps, to set him free.' Once more, a fusion of faith and love is achieved, in this sacrifice expressed through sexuality.

Another type of contrast to the Irish portrayal of Puritanism is the creation of characters who represent a perfect balance between human love and love of God. Mauriac, for example, in *L'Agneau* (1954), shows the saintly Xavier renouncing marriage in favour of other responsibilities, only because he 'always end(s) up preferring (Christ) to those (he) most love(s),' but not before he has fallen deeply in love with a woman.

In *Histoire d'un Bonheur*, Pierre-Henri Simon describes Noël Dussert's wife, Lucie, as representing an ideal synthesis of religious faith and a fully enjoyed sexual love. And when Nöel becomes a prisoner of war, she writes that if her hope of meeting him alive again is dashed, she will replace it with 'the hope . . . of another union of our beings, . . . in which the essence of our bodily love will burn eternally in the absolute fire of love.'

The theme of marital happiness in a Catholic context is in itself one which receives radically different types of treatment from our two groups of authors. Many of the French novelists describe aspirations to, and realisations of, a synthesis of faith and conjugal love absent from the works of the Irish.

Luc Estang, in *Que Ces Mots Répondent*, shows the Coltenceau couple progressing eventually to happiness. The hero of Mauriac's *L'Agneau* aspires, for a period, to the modest happiness of Christian marriage, and for one couple in *La Pharisienne* just such happiness springs from shared suffering. The protagonist of Maxence Van der Meersch's *Masque de Chair* believes strongly in the religious significance of marital sexuality. Some of Paul-André Lesort's characters discover this significance; in *Le Vent Souffle où il Veut* (1954), Yves owes his discovery of God and his conversion to Catholicism to the fact that the 'highest moments of their mutual joy, when their hearts, their bodies and their thoughts fuse like lava . . . light up . . . his whole life'. Guillaume

Périer likewise notes that 'At the supreme moments of love, time itself offers its own abolition. Glimmer of the Absolute.' And he goes on to write of marriage as a means of discovering God's love and as an 'eschatological witness of the kingdom of God.' Jacques de Bourbon Busset, in *Les Aveux Infidèles,* describes not only the discovery of faith through marital love, but also of the continuance and deepening of that love in the light of faith. Jean Sulivan in *Car Je t'aime, ô Eternité* (1960) describes sexual desire as an index of man's hunger for God, and Christian marriage as an authentic means of contact with eternity; he also affirms his knowledge of the 'miracle of successful friendship in marriage.'

On the Irish side, the first thing to note in considering the topic of Catholic marriage is the low incidence of married Catholics as central characters in the novels of the last few decades; approximately three out of every five protagonists are single, and about half the remainder are no longer Catholics. This is explained, at least in part, by a rather heavy concentration on the areas of childhood and adolescence on the part of autobiographically-inspired writers who were never married Catholics. In any case, the picture of Catholic marriage which emerges in Irish novels—through the portrayal of secondary as well as central characters—, is, in the main, a most unflattering one, with a constant insistence on the absence of sexual fulfilment and general happiness.

Brian Moore, for example, in *An Answer from Limbo*, has the widowed Mrs Tierney remember her husband's 'dislike of being kissed or touched'; she doubts whether she would have stayed with him had there been no laws to hold her. In *The Pilgrimage* (1961), John Broderick recounts Julia Glynn's exploits with two lovers after a disastrous marriage to a pious homosexual, whose attempt to reform his nature ends in brutality. In *An Apology for Roses* (1973), he tells how the heroine's mother, having banished her husband from her bed, remembers 'the first terrible years of their marriage when, a frigid woman, she had discovered with horror (his) insatiable appetite . . . it had been a nightmare.' Kevin

Casey, in *The Sinners' Bell* (1968), describes the first year of a marriage between two young Catholics; the consummation is a loveless ordeal, and before their first child is born, the husband's infidelity saps the wife's faith and happiness. Kate O'Brien's heroine in *That Lady* (1946), feels 'a great sense of waste in her long subjugation' to her husband, whose attempts to satisfy her sexually do little to bridge the gap between them. The heroine of Eilis Dillon's *Across the Bitter Sea* (1973) betrays her husband, and even when enjoying intimacy with him, imagines herself in the arms of her lover. A young wife in Thomas Kilroy's *The Big Chapel* finds herself always 'overcome by a kind of terror' in the sexual act. In *The Country Girls*, Edna O'Brien attributes Cait Brady's fear of sex to the fact that her mother 'had protested too agonisingly all through the windy years'; like the mother in Christy Brown's *Down all the Days*, she suffers from an alcoholic husband and wishes she had been a nun.

The exceptions to this pessimistic portrayal of Catholic marriage are slight. In *The Barracks*, Elizabeth Reegan feels grateful, at one point, for her husband's sexual attentions; I can think of nothing more positive, in this regard, in recent Irish novels. The couple involved, however, could not be said to represent ideal marital companionship strengthened by faith. Two of Walter Macken's heroes—in *The Silent People* (1962), and *Lord of the Mountain*—speak glowingly of their love for their wives; neither, though, is a practising Catholic, and one has deserted his wife for sixteen years.

An interesting gloss on the Irish authors' negative imagination as applied to human love can be found in Mervyn Wall's *Leaves for the Burning* (1952); the protagonist, Lucian Brewse Burke, observes a nun deal with a mentally ill patient who has lost her fiancé in an air crash, and reflects:

> Sacred and Profane Love . . . A nun's love is cool and professional. She serves the poor and the sick, a religious automaton with a face that isn't allowed emotion and a heart that is forbidden indignation . . . chill, dutiful,

christian love—how different from the rapture and tur-
moil of the other, profane love, often wicked: *at its
best, in the eyes of God, indifferent and without merit,*
in this case appositely brought to its close by a blazing
aeroplane and the torture of insanity (*emphasis added).*
A similar idea occurs in Kate O'Brien's novel, *The Land of Spices;*
the heroine, Helen Archer, is an exceptional character in the context of the Irish novel, insofar as, having entered a convent because of a sexual shock, she eventually tries 'to compromise with
human feeling'; nonetheless, while doing so, 'she admitted that
human love . . . must almost always offend the heavenly lover by
its fatuous egotism.' That word 'almost' is a concession, but one is
still at a few removes from the fusion of the two loves.

While on the subject of nuns, it is worth noting that, with the
further exception of Francis MacManus in *Flow on, Lovely River,*
no Irish novelist imagines a harmony of human feeling and love of
God either in a character's decision to enter a convent or in her
subsequent lifestyle. Contrasts to this can be found, for example,
in Pierre-Henri Simon's *Les Raisins Verts,* and in Jacques de
Bourbon Busset's *Le Silence et la Joie* (1957), in which the
widowed heroine bases her decision to become a Carmelite on the
belief in God she has acquired through the experience of married
love.

A few final odds and ends can serve to complete the study of
this aspect of our subject. Ex-seminarians in Irish novels are a
sorry sight. Padraig, in Richard Power's *The Land of Youth,* is
only one example of failure to adapt to secular living. Paddy
Flynn, in Kate O'Brien's *As Music and Splendour,* is another: 'the
puzzled half-would-be priest was not dead in him and, unin-
structed still as to the world, he feared its sins as he apprehended
them in himself and all about him—and he stared in dismay at the
human prospect.' Peter Fury, in James Hanley's *An End and a
Beginning,* suffers from being 'Another dismantled Roman wreck,
one more crashing priest,' and Nicholas Scully, in Thomas Kilroy's

The Big Chapel, is a 'Half-priest . . . Half-man . . . crippled by the Cross of Christ—not even the whole cross, only the shadow . . . '; voyeurism is his closest approach to sexual satisfaction. In contrast, Pierre-Henri Simon presents, in *Les Hommes ne Veulent pas Mourir,* an ex-seminarian who manages to find fulfilment and happiness in marriage. A partial exception in the Irish context occurs in Walter Macken's *Lord of the Mountain,* in which an ex-seminarian, generally unresponsive to women, decides to contract a celibate marriage with a mentally retarded girl in order to protect her. However, in *Car Je t'aime, ô Eternité,* Jean Sulivan refers to a choice of celibacy based on other aspects of love: a man and a woman find such joy and fulfilment in the consummation of their love that they decide to separate and direct towards others the capacity for self-giving which the experience has revealed to them. They make an interesting contrast not only to Macken's protective husband but to those fearful characters in flight from the flesh with whom we began our study of Puritanism.

'HANDLYNG SINNE'

Perhaps nowhere is the Irish-French contrast so striking as in the treatment of sexual sin.

The Irish writers, for the most part, describe those who decide or accept to live in sin as remaining divided, unable to resolve their conflict.

John Broderick, for example, in *The Pilgrimage,* shows the bi-sexual Stephen Lydon purchasing love at the expense of the disgust which sex occasions to his puritan nature and the guilt of which his genuinely pious mind remains acutely conscious. Broderick apparently sees no solution to his dilemma: Stephen affirms his readiness to remain in his mistress' employ even if a miracle were to make her paralysed homosexual husband a second source of disgust.

In *The Lonely Passion of Miss Judith Hearne,* Brian Moore portrays the elderly widower, James Madden, as perpetually divided, oscillating between sordid escapades and attacks of remorse; his religion involves an 'insurance' approach to confession but is too superficial to inspire any stable determination to reform.

Kate O'Brien, in *As Music and Splendour,* sees no solution to the dilemmas of her two heroines—Rose Lennane, who does 'nothing else but commit mortal sins—for sentimental reasons,' and Clare Halvey, a serious-minded lesbian for whom 'Life turns out to be an unceasing argument with conscience everywhere.' Reviewing their situations at the end of the novel, Clare reflects: 'Sin. The word came now from far enough away. Yet it was the word of all.'

Patrick Boyle's retelling of the Samson-Delilah story in *Like Any Other Man* (1966), contains a strong emphasis on Simpson's awareness of the sinfulness of his fornication, on his vain attempts to reform for his health's sake, and on his inability to face the ordeal of confession. Boyle widens rather than narrows the gap separating Simpson from a God imagined as essentially vindictive; the novel ends with the discovery of Simpson—syphilitic, blind, drunk, naked—amid the furniture that has crashed around the corpse of his strangled mistress.

The abyss dividing the hero of Kevin Casey's *The Sinners' Bell* from God is wider still. Frank Keenan, 'doomed to carry belief around with him like a birthmark,' thinks of sexual sin as the ideal way to express his independence of God; seducing a girl, 'He kissed her with hate . . . he could damn her soul for all eternity; the emotion was stronger and more violent than lust had ever been.' The opposition between sex and faith has rarely received such extreme expression.

Several of the French 'Catholic novelists' have shown themselves to be highly imaginative, not to say acrobatic, in finding solutions to the dilemma of the sexual sinner. An aspect of their approach already distinguishing them from Irish novelists is their portrayal of characters who have a deep intellectual grasp of their faith, and a strong *voluntary* attachment to it even while living in sin. And an initial index of their intent to reconcile opposites is their frequent portrayal of sin as a misdirection of a genuinely religious impulse. Pierre-Henri Simon, for example, has Laurent Seudre in *Le Somnambule* affirm that, in his adultery, 'I tried to prove to myself that, by an exceptional life involving risk, I still tended towards good.' Jean Sulivan's Serge Minardi in *Du Côté de l'Ombre* tries to 'mix pleasure and lofty moral aspirations.' In Béatrice Beck's *Léon Morin, Prêtre,* Barny's consent to lust takes the form of this inverted prayer: 'God, satisfy my desire just one single time, and then blessed be the eternal torment.' The hero of Julien Green's *Chaque Homme dans sa Nuit,* Wilfred Ingram, sins calmly only because he knows remorse will lead him to confess; his faith is stronger in places of pleasure than at Sunday Mass. The hero of Roger Bésus' *Le Refus* (1952) maintains that his visits to brothels are slender victories over a desire to visit churches. Paul-André Lesort and Luc Estang attribute to Michel Estienne and Octave Coltenceau a desire to re-create, through adultery, a lost earthly paradise.

Reconciliation of the sinner with God, in French novels, is frequent, its form somewhat varied. Whereas Irish writers, whether dealing with 'children in chains' or more rebellious sinners, are generally negative in their references to confession, some of the French are at times sufficiently orthodox to solve their characters' dilemmas by the normal means of straightforward repentance and recourse to the sacrament: Béatrice Beck, Paul-André Lesort, Luc Estang and Roger Bésus all portray protagonists overcoming a natural repugnance to the act by supernatural considerations; in the case of the first three, confession is followed by a resolute return to Christian living, while for Bésus' hero, it is the prelude to a saving death. Salvation is also accorded by Jean Sulivan to Serge Minardi, who dies before he can actualise the confession he has been rehearsing, and by Pierre-Henri Simon to Laurent Seudre. Julien Green is explicit about the salvation of Wilfred in *Chaque Homme dans sa Nuit* and of Karin in *L'Autre* (1971); though both experience a strong desire to confess, it is not sacramental confession which is the decisive factor in either case; for Wilfred, salvation is earned by the pardon he extends to his murderer, and for Karin it is guaranteed by a mystical experience. Similarly, Fabien, hero of Green's *Si J'Etais Vous,* dies in peace after a change of heart.

More striking than the reconciliation of the sinner with God, perhaps, is the reconciliation the French writers often envisage between the various elements of the sinner's conflict. Whereas the Irish novelists insist on their sinners' isolation and solitude, the French sometimes highlight a sinner's sense of solidarity with those who share his faith, and a supernatural concern for those who do not. Pierre-Henri Simon stresses Laurent Seudre's regret for the scandal caused by his adultery, and describes his attempts to exercise a Christian influence on non-believing acquaintances. When a nihilist friend tells Octave Coltenceau that Christians are unhappy, Octave feels he must 'protest; in the name of the *others!',* and proceeds to affirm his loyalty to Christ, in spite of his sin. Roger Bésus' hero, in *Le Refus,* tries to keep a couple from sin, saying he wishes to save them even if not himself. Mauriac's Alain Gajac brings an ex-seminarist back to his faith and his vocation, while living in sin himself. And Wilfred, in Green's *Chaque Homme dans sa Nuit,* prays for the deathbed conversion of an uncle whose dissolute life he is imitating, baptises a dying companion who wishes to share his faith, and undoes the apostasy he has caused in another friend.

A variation on this theme—uniting, in a way, all the elements of the conflict—occurs when the sinners try to convert their mistresses. In the case of the protagonist of a novella by Simon, *Celle Qui est née un Dimanche* (1952) adultery is the immediate consequence of such an attempt, and Sulivan's Serge Minardi preaches Christian morality only to advance his own sexual interests. Michel Estienne's approach, however, when breaking with his mistress, is more disinterested, and, in Julien Green's *L'Autre,* Roger's attempt—eventually successful—to convert Karin, whose faith he had destroyed ten years previously, is inspired at least partly by genuine concern. The same is true of Laurent Seudre's efforts to exert a beneficial influence on his nihilist mistress. His success is modest compared to that of Octave Coltenceau, who patiently catechizes his mistress so that she can share his sense of sin; she eventually understands so well that this is due to something bigger than either of them that she kills herself to set Octave free, explaining that his God should understand her self-giving.

Another way in which the authors we have been dealing with narrow the gap between sinner and God is to suggest the operation of grace on or through the sinner. Pierre-Henri Simon intimates that Laurent Seudre undergoes some mystical experience during his period of arid atonement. Michel Estienne believes he has been rescued from sin through the prayers of others. Mauriac, in *Un Adolescent d'Autrefois*, sees Alain Gajac and his seminarist friend gaining graces for each other and contributing to each other's salvation. And Julien Green's suggestion with regard to Wilfred Ingram's intervention in the lives of others is that he is unwittingly an instrument of God.

More striking still is the occasional evocation of the *felix culpa*, of sin as the occasion of grace. Luc Estang has Octave Coltenceau reflect on the paradox that a rebirth of love and happiness in his

marriage is the consequence of his adultery, and his spiritual director, commenting on Octave's suffering on the suicide of his mistress, says: 'Christ designed to associate you with his Passion—
through a passion!' Whereas Estang proposes such ideas *after* the
event, Roger Bésus seems far less orthodox in the timing of such
reflections. His hero, Dr Arnaud, takes a mistress—and later kills
her—in order to keep her from another man whom he wishes to
save from sin; he applies the notion of end justifying means to
murder as well as adultery: having killed the girl, he maintains he
has done so in order to hand her back to God, and as he goes to
hide the body, has the impression of carrying 'a little girl become
pure again, and over whom God watched.' Alain Gajac, in
Mauriac's *Un Adolescent d'Autrefois*, is so grateful for what he has
received from his mistress that, despite his attempt to achieve contrition, he 'felt this sin not as an offence but as a grace.' In Julien
Green's *L'Autre*, Karin's conversion is the consequence of Roger's
weakness in returning to her, and Green's implication, with regard
to the total action of the novel, is that the couple's dangerous
association bears fruit eventually in a *double* conversion.

A final nuance to be found in the works of some of the French
'Catholic novelists' is the presentation of the experience of illicit
love as the source of an intuition of the Absolute. Pierre-Henri
Simon hints at this idea a number of times in *Le Somnambule*.
Octave Coltenceau affirms that during his adulterous adventure, he
glimpsed the Beyond, lit up by the flame of passion. Mauriac is the
most explicit in hinting at a connection between this intuition and
the reconciliation of the sinner with God: if Alain Gajac looks on
his first night with his mistress as 'a night of sin and yet a night of
grace,' it is because

> That night we came closer than at any other time of
> our lives to the truth we both suspected . . . that human
> love is the prefiguration of the love which created us,—
> but that sometimes, as for us on that night, despite its
> sinfulness, it resembled that love of the Creator for the

creature and of the creature for the Creator, and that the happiness with which Marie and I overflowed was like a pardon granted in advance.

EXCEPTIONS

At this point, having stressed the totally different approaches of the French and Irish writers, it is appropriate to comment on the extent and importance of apparent or partial exceptions among the latter.

With regard to the topic we have just been dealing with, for example, it is interesting to note that Kate O'Brien, in two of her novels, speaks of the experience of sinful love in terms that recall the French writers' references to its absolute dimension. Rose Lennane, in *As Music and Splendour*, maintains, of her first experience of love: 'It was a sin, . . .but it had been and still could be, a blessed and irresistible experience, a true explanation of life, for better or worse', and the adulterous Ana de Mendoza, heroine of *That Lady*, addressing her conscience, says: 'so be it . . . I am living in sin. But I've found something that has been missing always, and that may indeed be just as important as what your voice tells me of.' Rose, however, is not reconciled to God, and though Kate O'Brien charts Ana's eventual spiritual progress, she insists on her inability, for reasons of intellectual honesty, to be truly repentant. The resolution of the contradiction would appear to lie in the notion—put forward by a cardinal, a friend of Ana's —of a God not 'all made of tiny rules and calculations,' but Ana appears never to accept the Cardinal's supplementary notion that 'It's not such a very long journey from the love of man to the love of God.'

In Eilis Dillon's *Across the Bitter Sea*, the heroine tells her lover, after her husband's death: 'I used to curse love, and think it was a disease, . . . but I don't think that now. Every love has good in it, no matter how it breaks the law of God or man afterward . . . ' This 'good', however, is seen in terms of human happiness only; that there is no suggestion of a *felix culpa* becoming an occasion for the operation of grace is proved by the confused and superficial understanding of morality, sin, and confession, on the part of heroine, husband, and lover.

John Broderick, in *An Apology for Roses*, describes a priest's decision, after an affair with a young woman, to remain faithful to his vocation. His behaviour at the moment of separation—when he asks the girl not to infer from his conduct that 'everything in life is a bit of a humbug'— resembles that of some of the protagonists in French novels. His attitude to confession is a simple one, and it is to be presumed that he avails himself of the sacrament, for he is soon to be seen trying to follow his parish priest's advice as to how to persevere in his vocation. Broderick, however, using the parish priest as his spokesman, pours scorn on the idea of sexual sin as *felix culpa*: 'That . . . is a load of shit. . . . That human love . . . which we're supposed to be always preaching about . . . is neither romantic nor passionate, it's acceptance of yourself and other people . . . . Any other interpretation of what we do is not only heresy, it's drooling nonsense.'

The desire to reconcile opposites, then, by suggesting that sexual sin can be 'used' by God to give grace, is not a feature of the Irish novelists' approach. And wherever there is the suggestion of a divine intervention—as there is in Broderick's *The Pilgrimage* and Walter Macken's *Sunset on the Window-Panes*

(1954) and possibly in Richard Power's *The Land of Youth*—it operates entirely independently of sexual love, sinful or holy. There are other Irish novels, which, if written in France, might earn their authors the title of 'Catholic novelist', but the writers' faith is sometimes apparent from a direct authorial comment, sometimes deducible from the depth and intensity of interest with which certain questions are approached—this seems to me the case with Gerald Hanley's *Without Love* and Richard Power's *The Hungry Grass* (1969).

There is, however, one manifestation of a 'positive imagination' which some Irish novelists have in common with the French, and that is the affirmation that certain interpersonal (but non-sexual) relationships can have a beneficial effect on the faith of an individual. This idea is given brief and near-symbolic expression by Walter Macken at one point in *The Silent People*, where a despairing priest is encouraged by a chance encounter with a fellow-priest. Similarly, as noted previously, John Broderick, in *An Apology for Roses*, shows a parish priest helping his curate to persevere, and in *The Greatest of These* (1943) Francis MacManus attributes a rebel priest's submission to the charity shown by his bishop. In *That Lady*, Kate O'Brien seems to account for her heroine's spiritual progress by the prayer of others and the Communion of Saints. *The Land of Spices* also may be thought of as an imaginative exposition of this doctrine, portraying as it does the mutually beneficial effect of a friendship between a nun and one of her charges. (The same novel may also contain an indirect hint at the *felix culpa* idea, since the nun's dedication is ultimately a result of her pagan father's homosexuality.)

The only Irish novelist I know of who puts forward the ideal of a blend of friendship, sexuality and faith in Christ is Francis Stuart. The hero of his *The Pillar of Cloud* (1948), Dominic Malone, has a strong faith in Christ, and a special regard for 'fraternity with a woman.' For altruistic reasons, Dominic marries the younger sister of the girl he loves, having first converted her by reading to her the story of Mary Magdalen, and he experiences physical union with her both as sacrifice and purification. When she dies, he is free to indulge his love for the older girl, and, in describing this love, Stuart resorts to biblical language to render the sense of a mystical experience rooted in the physical.

> ... life was being given to them. They felt it being poured into them, into their bosoms from a measure full and running over. ... There was no division into sensual and spiritual. There was no division or weighing or measure. The measure in which life was given to them was running over, always full and overflowing so that they were filled and fulfilled.

However, though the context of this mystical love is Christian, it is not Catholic; the couple do not marry, as institutional religion leaves them cold. Stuart seems to regard the official Church as incapable of fostering such love as he portrays.

QUESTIONS AND EXPLANATIONS

We began this study with the observation that no one speaks of Irish 'Catholic novelists'. One possible reason I put forward is that Irish writers who remain Catholic fail to distinguish themselves significantly from their ex-Catholic compatriots; by sharing with the latter a 'negative imagination' with regard to certain basic themes, they are deprived of a particular source of inspiration which many French novelists have exploited with striking affect.

However, I feel it only fair to say at this point that I suspect that the non-emergence, to any notable degree, of an Irish 'Catholic novel', may have something to do with statistics and voluntary stance, as well as with imaginative disposition. Several of the French novelists we have studied speak of their work as constituting a conscious witness to the faith and this seems to me not unconnected with their consciousness of writing for a de-Christianised public. Conversely, I have the impression that some of the Irish novelists might be more 'Catholic' if more of their compatriots were less so. In a society composed overwhelmingly of practising Catholics, it is perhaps natural that even those writers best disposed towards Catholicism should aim less at charting the (supposedly familiar) advantages of virtue or repentance than at chronicling instances of that hypocrisy, mediocrity and intolerance which are likely to be found in any community menaced by complacency. (A corollary to this theory would be that an Irish Bernanos or Mauriac may yet arise, in reaction to those secularist influences which are undoubtedly gaining ground in Irish society.)

But to return to the 'negative imagination', which is our chief concern. Behind it lies, it seems obvious, 'negative experience', either personal or observed. A comment on one or two aspects of this might be in order.

Several Irish novelists, as we have seen, attribute defections from the faith to oppressive authority and intolerant attitudes. In this they are doubtless reflecting a genuine social reality which transcends their personal experience, so that their accounts have a paradigmatic as well as the autobiographical dimension noted by critics. 'The *non serviam* of Irish writers does not necessarily come out of thin air; the society itself is often partially responsible . . .', writes Augustine Martin. 'The cost of salvation is high when one lacks pastoral understanding. It has been too high for too many (Irish writers)', says one priest-critic. And another comments:

' . . . Many have left the fold, driven out, no doubt, by inner tensions which they failed to resolve, but which could, perhaps, have been resolved by a more sympathetic attitude of the part of the Church'.

It may be noted, of course, that the extreme consequences of such lack of understanding indicate an imperfectly grasped faith on the part of the victims, and this too would appear to correspond to an aspect of the Irish reality. Commenting on socially-based Irish religious practice endangered by emigration, J.K. Pollard notes: 'Faith is, in many ways, a cultural expression. It does not have that "intellectual" or, better, intelligent basis needed to survive, much less convert the alien, pluralist society outside Ireland'. If one looks for a historical reason for the over-emphasis on authority and the weakness of the doctrinal basis for practice (which, though not the whole Irish picture, are undoubted features of it), Sean O'Faolain's perhaps simplistic explanation may be worth considering:

> . . . When we lost our native aristocracy after the Williamite wars (1691), but still held firmly to our traditional faith, we were left with a purely popular or peasant church much too poor and too harassed to develop an intellectual life either among its priests or its people. In the circumstances, the Church, not unnaturally, found it easier to rule by command rather than by advice or persuasion.

On the question of the general inability of Irish writers to envisage a harmonious relationship between sexuality and religion, it would be generally acknowledged, I think, that this in some way reflects the existence of certain inhibiting attitudes towards sex, which were a feature of some sectors of Irish Catholic life. Variously described as Jansenism or Puritanism, this phenomenon is most often attributed to a rigid clerically-inspired education. Much polemical ink has been expended on this subject, and allowance must be made for a sense of personal grievance on the part of many commentators. However, a recent joint pastoral by the Irish bishops recognises (though without specific reference to the Irish context) the existence of erroneous views of sex, and implicitly puts part of the blame on narrow-minded moralists. In any case it appears clear that a negative education in matters pertaining to sexuality has left its mark on many Irish authors, contributing to the total disenchantment with the Church on the part of some, and leaving others equally unable to envisage a healthy integration of sex and faith.

Having said all this, we might remind ourselves that many of the French writers we have studied take the same basic problem of oppressive authority and sexual malaise as the starting-point for their eventually more optimistic propositions, and we might wonder what are the features of the French Catholic climate which could account for their 'positive imagination'. An aspect of this 'positive imagination' is the portrayal of a faith which draws resilience from its intellectual, or at least intelligent character. This undoubtedly reflects the authors' own stance, and that of a great many French practising Catholics, whose practice, in a predominantly secularist environment, must owe less to social conformity than to intellectual conviction. The statistical factor is, as we have seen, important. Indeed it can be argued—there is evidence for it in the writings of Bloy, Claudel and Maritain—that it was precisely the anti-spiritual bias of the French intellectual establishment at the turn of the century which called forth, in reaction, the Catholic Revival inspired largely by intellectual laymen. This movement, for which there is, of course, no Irish parallel, can be credited with the propagation of a rigorously intelligent approach to religious doctrine; involving no real distinction between thinker and creative writer, its influence has extended through men like Gilson, Mounier, Daniel-Rops, Bernanos, Mauriac and others down to our own day. It is this tradition that the writers we have studied inherit and perpetuate.

Their participation in this tradition is perhaps particularly clear in their positive treatment of sexuality and marriage. A preliminary clarification is needed here: lest it be thought that Ireland has or had a monopoly of narrow views in this area, let me quote a theologian who, writing in 1947, was concerned with the Catholic world generally, and was better acquainted with the French than with the Irish scene:

> In our day the idea still persists in ecclesiastical and religious circles that marriage cannot be separated from "impurity", to such an extent that many would regard the expression "conjugal chastity" as something of an enigma. An impression is given that marriage and chastity are opposed; the essential of marriage seems to be the permission no longer to be chaste.

However, the same author goes on to say that 'certain circumstances proper to the age' have brought about in the Church a deeper appreciation of the sanctity of marriage:

> Nowadays the doctrines of the right to free love place before us as a formula for human perfection a system giving full liberty to the life of the passions, and the married Christian, when in contact with the modern world, feels that his life exacts sacrifices from him. In order to consent to these sacrifices, he must understand the high quality of the ideal which he follows . . . The theologian is thus stimulated . . . to work out the theology of the sacrament of marriage and to find out wherein lies its truly divine character.

The advocates of free love have undoubtedly been more vocal in France than in Ireland (until very recently at least); it is not surprising then, if one accepts Leclercq's thesis, that French thinkers have been to the fore in promoting a deeper understanding of Christian marriage. Bishop Cahal Daly, noting that 'the Catholic philosophy and spirituality of marriage have been developed *chiefly by laymen*', pays tribute to a host of Frenchmen—Maurice Blondel, Jacques Maritain, Jean Guitton, Gabriel Madinier, Gabriel

Marcel, Emmanuel Mounier, Jean Lacroix, Paul Archambault, Joseph Vialatoux, Gustave Thibon, Emmanuel Gounot, René Biot, Dr Sutter, Dr Le Moal, and Dr Paul Chauchard. And he makes the interesting point that such 'proponents of the natural law philosophy and morality of sex and marriage have grounded their case . . . on the nature of human love'. With such influences at work in Catholic circles in France, it is easier to understand how novelists like Simon, Lesort, Busset and others who explore human love can provide an imaginative exposition of theological ideas which constitute both a contrast to non-Christian thinking and a corrective to a less comprehensive Catholic spirituality.

A final comment: if the French scene appears to provide a healthier relationship between dogma and literature than that which obtains in Ireland, the sociological 'explanations' of this phenomenon call for a broad application—to societies as well as scribes—of Sterne's celebrated sentence, which aptly summarizes my findings and my feelings: 'They order, said I, this matter better in France'.

NOTES

Pages 11-12: Cf. John Jordan, 'Neglected Areas', *Hibernia*, 5 February, 1971; Sean O'Faolain, 'Fifty Years of Irish Writing', *Studies*, Spring 1962, pp. 101-102; Michael Sheehy, *Is Ireland Dying?: Culture and the Church in Modern Ireland*, London 1968, pp. 21-22 and 106; Graham Greene, *In Search of a Character*, London 1961, p. 24 of Penguin edition, 1968; John Broderick, 'Of Gods and English Gentlemen', *Hibernia*, 18 January 1974; John Broderick, *Hibernia*, 3 November 1972; Sallie Sears, *The Negative Imagination* (New York 1968).

Page 13 and passim: Throughout this book on first mention of a novel the date of first publication follows in parentheses; at the end is a list, by author, of the novels cited.

Page 26: Cf. Joseph K. Pollard, *The Pastoral Dimension of Contemporary Anglo-Irish Literature*, Rome 1970, p. 28.

Page 34, line 17: 'Coffey will always see Father Cogley (clearly . . . his most cogent perception of the Church) taunting his human endeavours . . . and he will always . . . in all he strives to achieve, work in order to disprove the conscious remembrance of the Father Cogley-Church-Bully' (Pollard, *op. cit.*, p. 28).

Page 36, line 2: John Broderick notes, for example, Hugh Ward's awareness that the hoped-for 'shining city' never materializes (*The Fugitives*, p. 143) and James Hanley has it remarked of the socialist Desmond Fury: 'He was going to turn the whole bloody world into a trade union, and was only angry with God Almighty because he couldn't give *Him* a union card too' (*An End and a Beginning*, p. 248). Such elements, we may notice in passing, are absent from the treatment of those French characters whose faith is totally dead; neither Luc Estang nor Paul-André Lesort suggests that Serge Demonin or Fernand Drouet pursues, with hate, a cause doomed to frustration.

Page 55, line 11: Cf. Julien Green, *L'Autre*, p. 461; also Julien Green, *Ce Qui Reste de Jour*, p. 269, and Ada Carella, 'Qui est l'Autre pour Julien Green?', *Le Cri du Monde*, May 1971, pp. 50-51.

Page 55, line 21: Cf. *The Lonely Passion of Miss Judith Hearne* (Penguin edition), pp. 40, 43, 48; *As Music and Splendour*, pp. 260, 312-313; *The Pilgrimage* (Pan edition), p. 101; *The Sinners' Bell*, p. 221.

Page 60, line 5: Cf. Patrick Kavanagh, *Tarry Flynn* (Mayflower edition), p. 92, and Walter Macken, *Lord of the Mountain*, p. 183.

Page 62, line 7: Cf. Mauriac: note written for P.H. Simon, *Mauriac par lui-même*, (Paris 1970), p. 58; Julien Green, *Journal 1949-1966* (Paris 1969); p. 1051; P.H. Simon, *Ce Que Je Crois* (Paris 1966), p. 185; Luc Estang, *Ce Que Je Crois* (Paris 1956), pp. 11-12; Jacques de Bourbon Busset, *Complices* (Paris 1974), p. 143; Jean Sulivan, *Miroir Brisé* (Paris 1969), p. 52.

Page 62, line 10: Cf. a remark by Mauriac quoted in Michel Paleotti, *Civilisation Française Contemporaine* (Paris 1973), p. 24; Julien Green, *Journal 1928-1949* (Paris 1969), pp. 753-754, and *Journal 1949-1966*, pp. 1416 and 1454; P.H. Simon, *Ce Que Je Crois*, pp. 184 and 209.

Page 62, line 18: This would appear, for example, to be the attitude to which John Broderick gave ironic expression on receiving the Irish Academy of Letters Award on 26 January 1976; 'Politicians and the Bishops usually accept awards on behalf of their constituency or diocese .... I accept on behalf of the salubrious, chaste, charitable and deeply religious town of Athlone, without which I'd never have written my books' *Irish Times,* 27 January 1976; *Irish Press,* same date).

Page 62, line 32: Augustine Martin, 'Inherited Dissent: The Dilemma of the Irish Writer', *Studies,* Spring 1965, p. 19.

Page 62, line 34: J.K. Pollard, *op. cit.,* p. 69.

Page 63, line 4: Thomas Halton, 'The Catholic Writer', October 1957, *Christus Rex,* p. 708.

Page 63, line 13: J.K. Pollard, *op. cit.,* p. 58.

Page 63: Sean O'Faolain, *The Irish* (Pelican edition) 1969, p. 119.

Page 64: 'The sexual aspect of marriage has sometimes been feared by some or endured by others as a condition of marriage ... Too few see it as something good and holy in marriage, blessed by the sacrament and sanctifying the partners': *Human Life is Sacred,* par. 82 (Dublin 1975). And: 'Marriage was sometimes discussed by moralists mainly in terms of "marriage rights". This would be a very limited view of the matter ...' (*ibid.*)

Page 65, lines 13 and 26: Jacques Leclercq, *Le Mariage Chrétien,* translated by the Earl of Wicklow as *Marriage a Great Sacrament* (Dublin 1951), pp. 24-25.

Page 65, line 33 and page 66, line 6: Cahal B. Daly, *Natural Law Morality Today* (Dublin 1965), p. 29.

Page 66, line 18: Laurence Sterne, *A Sentimental Journey,* 1, i.

BIBLIOGRAPHY: Novels mentioned in the text

Beck, Béatrice: Barny (Paris 1948)
    Léon Morin, Prêtre (Paris 1952)
Bésus, Roger: Le Refus (Paris 1952)
Boyle, Patrick: Like Any Other Man (London 1965)
Broderick, John: The Fugitives (London 1962)
    The Waking of Willie Ryan (London 1965)

Broderick, John (contd.)
  The Pilgrimage (London 1961)
  An Apology for Roses (London 1973)
Brown, Christy: Down All the Days (London 1970)
de Bourbon Busset, Jacques: Les Aveux Infidèles (Paris 1962)
  Le Silence et la Joie (Paris 1957)
Casey, Kevin: The Sinners' Bell (London 1968)
Dillon, Eilis: Bold John Henebry (London 1965)
  Across the Bitter Sea (London 1973)
Estang, Luc: Le Bonheur et le Salut (Paris 1961)
  Que Ces Mots Répondent (Paris 1964)
Farrell, Michael: Thy Tears Might Cease (London 1963)
Green, Julien: Si J'Etais Vous (Paris 1947)
  Chaque Homme dans sa Nuit (Paris 1960)
  L'Autre (Paris 1971)
Hanley, Gerald:Drinkers of Darkness (London 1955)
  Without Love (London 1957)
Hanley, James: An End and a Beginning (London 1957)
  Winter Song (London 1950)
Kavanagh, Patrick: Tarry Flynn (London 1948)
Kennelly, Patrick: Sausages for Tuesday (Dublin 1969)
Kiely, Benedict: Call for a Miracle (London 1950)
Kilroy, Thomas: The Big Chapel (London 1971)
Lesort, Paul-André: Les Reins et les Coeurs (Paris 1946)
  Vie de Guillaume Périer (Paris 1966)
  Le Vent Souffle Où Il Veut (Paris 1954)
McGahern, John: The Dark (London 1965)
  The Barracks (London 1963)
Macken, Walter: Brown Lord of the Mountain (London 1967)
  The Silent People (London 1962)
  Sunset on the Windowpanes (New York 1954)
MacManus, Francis: The Fire in the Dust (New York 1951)
  Flow on Lovely River (Dublin 1941)
  The Greatest of These (Dublin 1943)
Mauriac, Francois: Le Sagouin (Paris 1951)
  La Pharisienne (Paris 1941)

Mauriac, François (contd.)
  L'Agneau (Paris 1954)
  Un Adolescent d'Autrefois (Paris 1969)
Moore, Brian: A Moment of Love [originally The Feast
  of Lupercal] (London 1958)
    The Emperor of Ice-Cream (London 1965)
    The Luck of Ginger Coffey (London 1960)
    The Lonely Passion of Miss Judith Hearne (London 1955)
    I am Mary Dunne (London 1968)
    Fergus (London 1971)
    An Answer from Limbo (New York 1962)
Naughton, Bill: One Small Boy (London 1957)
O'Brien, Edna: A Pagan Place (London 1970)
    The Country Girls (London 1960)
    Girl with Green Eyes [originally The Lonely Girl] (London 1962)
    Girls in their Married Bliss (London 1964)
    August is a Wicked Month (London 1965)
O'Brien, Kate: The Last of Summer (London 1943)
    The Land of Spices (London 1941)
    As Music and Splendour (London 1958)
    That Lady (London 1946)
Power, Richard: The Land of Youth (London 1966)
    The Hungry Grass (London 1969)
Saint Pierre, Michael de: Ce Monde Ancien! (Paris 1948)
Simon, Pierre-Henri: Le Somnambule (Paris 1961)
    Les Raisins Verts (Paris 1950)
    Les Hommes ne Veulent pas Mourir (Paris 1953)
    Histoire d'un Bonheur (Paris 1965)
    La Sagesse du Soir (Paris 1971)
    Celle Qui est née un Dimanche (Neuchâtel 1952)
Smith, Paul: Stravaganza (London 1963)
Stuart, Francis: The Pillar of Cloud (London 1948)
Sulivan, Jean: Du Côté de l'Ombre (Paris 1962)
    Car Je t'aime, ô Eternité (Paris 1966)
Van der Meersch, Maxence: Masque de Chair (Paris 1958)
Wall, Mervyn: Leaves for the Burning (London 1952)

INDEX [of novelists cited]

THIS BOOK is a study of Irish novels between the years 1941 and 1973 in their most typical aspect—a pull. and drag between sex and religion, between morality and faith. Dr O'Rourke compares a wide range of Irish novelists with selected French contemporaries, arriving at the conclusion that 'they order this matter better in France'. . .

Brian O'Rourke was born in Ratheniska, county Laois, in 1948. He graduated in arts with first class honours at University College, Galway in 1969 and took a doctorate in comparative literature at the University of the New Sorbonne in 1976. He lectured in UCG in 1973-74 and since then has taught Complementary Studies at the Regional Technical College, Galway.